7 KEY WAYS TO UNLOCK THE INFINITE POTENTIAL OF YOUR THERAPY PRACTICE WITH DIGITAL CONTENT:

Build relationships. Share knowledge. Transform lives.

Ramon Antonio Matta

Content Done Write

CONTENTS

7 KEY WAYS TO UNLOCK THE INFINITE POTENTIAL OF YOUR THERAPY PRACTICE WITH DIGITAL CONTENT:

Build relationships.
Share knowledge.
Transform lives.

INTRODUCTION

The digital age has transformed therapy practices, enabling therapists to connect with a diverse and vast audience. Online or teletherapy has gained popularity, allowing therapists to communicate with patients using video calls, phone conversations, and text messaging. Digital tools have streamlined record-keeping, appointment scheduling, and client management, making therapy more efficient.

Therapists can access various educational materials, webinars, and online courses, broadening their horizons and engaging with global professional communities. The digital realm has also given rise to a vibrant international community of therapists passionate about helping others. **Digital content is crucial in therapy practices, educating clients, enhancing credibility, and creating a solid online presence.** Consistently publishing content and using strategic search engine optimization (SEO) strategies can enrich a therapist's online presence and make it easily accessible to potential clients.

Interactive digital content has revolutionized how therapists connect with their clients, fostering meaningful engagement. Webinars, podcasts, and social media posts have become powerful tools for disseminating knowledge, allowing clients to engage in real-time discussions and share valuable insights. Personalization has emerged as a versatile tool, enabling therapists to forge meaningful connections with diverse populations.

Digital apps have emerged as a practical solution to bridge the gap between traditional therapy and the modern digital landscape, empowering individuals to take charge of their well-being.

However, therapists must be competent in utilizing digital tools to enhance their practice. *Digital content can improve therapy delivery, allowing therapists to connect with patients unprecedentedly and transcend physical boundaries.* It also has the remarkable ability to boost patient adherence, a crucial aspect of successful therapy.

This book aims to showcase and examine the various types of digital content that therapists can use to improve their therapy practice, strengthen their relationships with clients, attract a broader audience to demonstrate their expertise, and educate, ultimately benefiting their practice.

UNDERSTANDING DIGITAL CONTENT

The digital landscape is a vast collection of information, communication, and entertainment, which includes various mediums like written content, social media posts, blog articles, and email newsletters. It also involves visual and auditory elements like images and videos and interactive features like quizzes and games. In psychotherapy, blogs prove to be a powerful tool for therapists to share insights and experiences and connect with clients and potential clients.

E-books are comprehensive guides that enable readers to explore various aspects of psychotherapy at their own pace. Videos and podcasts have also emerged as powerful tools for sharing knowledge, particularly in mental health. Videos have revolutionized how people consume information, offering a dynamic and engaging experience. Additionally, webinars and online workshops have transformed how people learn and engage with experts in various areas.

Social media posts and infographics have broadened our scope, allowing us to connect with a vast and diverse audience. Digital content has become the key to informing, engaging, and influencing a specific audience in this ever-evolving digital landscape.

Digital content connects clients with valuable resources and inspirational content, breaking down barriers and connecting people from around the globe. It is also integral to psychotherapy practices, providing information and support to individuals seeking guidance and understanding *Furthermore, digital content has been used to extend the boundaries of mental health interventions, disseminate invaluable information, and foster community resilience and well-being.* By harnessing the power of technology, we can create a better-informed society and more compassionate towards mental health.

DIGITAL CONTENT STRATEGY

A well-thought-out digital content strategy is essential for therapy practices. It streamlines the content creation process, allowing for the efficient use of resources. By understanding the audience's desires, needs, and aspirations, content can be tailored to resonate with them.

A content audit helps identify strengths and weaknesses, while planning involves mapping out the journey, envisioning topics, and determining the formats that best captivate the audience. The content strategy also consists of selecting the channels through which it is distributed, such as social media platforms or email newsletters. By discerning the ideal form of digital content that aligns with the objectives, therapy practices can effectively engage clients and deliver mental health resources, impacting their mental health journey.

In today's digital age, selecting the most appropriate digital channels and platforms for content distribution to reach the intended audience is crucial. Each platform has its unique benefits, and it is essential to consider the target audience's characteristics and align them with the strengths of each channel. **A well-planned digital content strategy is critical for therapy**

practices to navigate the digital landscape and provide unwavering client support effectively.

A content strategy establishes clear goals, identifies the right content types, selects appropriate media, and implements efficient production processes to ensure digital resources perfectly align with the practice's objectives and clients' needs. By understanding their preferences and habits, therapy practices can deliver their message in a way that resonates with their target audience and engages them on a deeper level.

Creating a Content Strategy for a Therapy Practice:

1. Define Your Goals: What do you want to achieve with your content? This could be anything from increasing your online presence, attracting new clients, providing resources for existing clients, or positioning yourself as an expert in your field.

2. Understand Your Audience: Who are you creating content for? Understanding your clients' needs, interests, and challenges will help you create content that resonates with them.

3. Conduct a Content Audit: Evaluate your existing content. What types of content are performing well? What gaps exist in your current content?

4. Plan Your Content: Based on your goals and your audience's needs, plan the types of content you'll create. This could include blog posts, podcasts, social media updates, e-books, etc.

5. Create a Content Calendar: An editorial calendar helps you plan what content to publish, when, and where. It ensures regular and consistent content creation and distribution.

6. Develop Your Content: With your plan in place, start creating your content. Ensure each piece is high-quality, engaging, and aligns with your brand voice.

7.   **Distribute and Promote:** Decide where and how you'll share your content. This could be on your website, social media platforms, email newsletters, etc.

8.   **Measure and Refine:** Use analytics to track the performance of your content. This will help you understand what's working and what's not and how to improve.

A successful content strategy is not set in stone. It requires regular review and adjustment based on your evolving goals, audience needs, and content performance.

7 WAYS TO USE DIGITAL CONTENT TO ENHANCE A THERAPY PRACTICE

Stepping into the dynamic world of mental health care, therapists are ceaselessly searching for fresh, inventive methods to elevate their practice and enrich their clients' journeys. Amidst the digital revolution, one tool stands out with a resounding impact—content.

Digital content, from enlightening blog posts and comprehensive e-books to engaging podcasts and insightful social media posts, unfurls untapped potential for connection, education, and empowerment.

This guide peels back the layers of seven powerful digital content forms readily available for therapists to weave into their practice. With these tools, mental health professionals can amplify their visibility, cultivate profound connections with clients, and enhance their services in ways previously unimagined.

Whether you've been in the field for years or just starting your journey, these valuable insights will arm you with practical strategies, helping you leave a lasting digital footprint and transform your practice.

WAY 1: BLOGS

Snapshot:

In the context of a therapy practice, blogs can significantly contribute to its growth and client engagement. They offer a platform for therapists to share expert insights, therapeutic techniques, and helpful resources, fostering a deeper understanding of mental health topics among readers. By consistently publishing blog posts, therapists can establish themselves as authorities in their field, building trust and credibility with their audience.

Blogs also provide an opportunity to humanize the practice, sharing personal stories or client success stories (with permission, maintaining confidentiality). They can also serve as a platform for open discussion, encouraging readers to share their thoughts or experiences, thereby fostering a sense of community.

Incorporating a blog into a therapy practice can increase visibility, client engagement, and a more informed and empowered clientele.

Deep Focus: Developing Engaging Blog Content

The importance of blogging for therapists lies in its potential to provide a platform for self-reflection, knowledge sharing, and professional development, ultimately enhancing therapy practices. To achieve this, therapists should identify their target audience and the specific goals they aim to achieve through the blog. These goals include providing educational resources, sharing personal reflections, or offering insights into therapeutic techniques.

Choosing a suitable platform for hosting a blog is essential to ensure that it aligns with the therapist's branding and provides the necessary features for content creation and engagement with readers.

Regarding content creation, therapists can write about various topics, including mental health tips, coping strategies, personal reflections on therapy sessions, discussions on mental health issues, and insights into therapeutic approaches. Additionally, therapists can use their blogs to share success stories, relevant research findings, and practical resources that benefit their clients and the broader community.

Therapists need to maintain a professional and ethical approach in their blogging. They must ensure the content is accurate, respectful, and aligned with ethical guidelines in therapy practices.

Therapists can encourage client engagement by allowing comments on their blog posts, responding to inquiries, and fostering a sense of community through their online platform. This contributes to building a supportive and informative space for clients to access valuable mental health resources and engage in meaningful discussions.

Deeper Focus: Optimizing Blogs for Success

Blogs effectively allow therapists to share their insights,

educate clients, and establish their online presence. They provide a unique platform to discuss various topics related to mental health, therapy techniques, and self-improvement, which can be valuable resources for clients and potential clients.

Importance of Blogging for Therapists:

- Engagement: Blogs allow therapists to engage with their audience meaningfully. They can address common concerns, answer questions, and facilitate mental health discussions.

- Authority: Regularly publishing well-researched and insightful blog posts helps establish a therapist as an authority in their field. This can build credibility and trust with clients.

- SEO: Search engines favor websites with regularly updated, relevant content. Blogging can significantly improve a therapist's visibility on search engine results, making it easier for potential clients to discover their services.

- Connection: Sharing personal experiences, insights, and stories can help therapists connect more deeply with their audience and foster a sense of community and belonging among readers.

Starting a Blog:

1. **Choose a Platform:** There are many blogging platforms available, such as WordPress, Blogger, or Squarespace. Choose one that best meets your needs regarding functionality, ease of use, and cost.

2. **Define Your Niche:** Identify the specific areas within therapy or mental health that you want to focus on. This could be based on your specialization, places of interest, or

the needs of your target audience.

3.   **Plan Your Content:** Create a content plan outlining the topics you want to cover, the frequency of posts, and the keywords to target for SEO.

4.   **Write and Publish:** Start writing your blog posts. Please make sure they are well-researched, easy to read, and provide value to your audience. Use images, headers, and bullet points to make your content more digestible.

5.   **Promote:** Share your blog posts on your website, social media platforms, and email newsletters. Encourage your audience to share them, too.

What to Write About:

- **Mental Health Awareness:** Write about different mental health conditions, symptoms, and treatment options.
- **Therapy Techniques:** Explain other therapy techniques and how they can help clients.
- **Self-Care Tips:** Provide tips on self-care and coping strategies for managing stress, anxiety, or depression.
- **Success Stories:** With their permission, share the success stories of clients who have benefited from therapy.
- **Q&A Posts:** Answer common questions about treatment or mental health.
- **Latest Research:** Discuss the latest research in mental health and therapeutic care.

Blogging is a long-term commitment. Consistency, quality, and relevance are vital to running a successful blog.

WAY 2: E-BOOKS

Snapshot:

E-books can be invaluable in enhancing a therapy practice, transforming how therapists share knowledge and connect with their clients. By creating and distributing e-books on various aspects of mental health, therapists can provide comprehensive, accessible resources that clients can refer to outside of therapy sessions. This supplements the therapy process and empowers clients by giving them tools and insights to navigate their mental health journey.

Moreover, e-books can showcase a therapist's expertise and thought leadership, attracting potential clients and establishing credibility. E-books offer a unique blend of education, engagement, and outreach, making them a powerful addition to any therapy practice's digital content strategy.

Deep Focus: Organizing Content in E-books

To organize content in e-books, therapists should aim for clarity and conciseness. They should structure the content with chapters or sections, add visual elements like images, infographics, diagrams, interactive features like quizzes, worksheets, or self-reflection prompts, and provide references for further exploration. The goal of each e-book should be to provide value to clients, enhancing their therapy experience and supporting their mental health journey.

Therapists can create e-books on various topics relevant to therapy practice, including coping strategies, mental health education, mindfulness exercises, self-care techniques, and psychoeducational resources.

The format of e-books for therapy practice may vary, encompassing informative guides, interactive workbooks, self-help manuals, and resource compilations that cater to clients' diverse needs and preferences. Therapists can also incorporate multimedia elements such as videos, audio recordings, and interactive exercises to enhance the engagement and effectiveness of the e-book content.

To start an e-book for therapy practice, therapists should identify the target audience's specific needs and interests, determine the e-book's key objectives, and select a suitable format and platform for content creation and distribution.

They should ensure that the eBook content aligns with ethical guidelines, respects client confidentiality, and provides accurate and evidence-based information to support clients' well-being.

Deeper Focus: Designing E-books for Engagement and Learning

Unlike blogs or social media posts, e-books enable therapists to delve into a subject more thoroughly and provide a valuable resource that clients can refer to repeatedly.

Benefits of Creating E-books for Therapy Clients:

- **Authority:** Publishing an e-book on a topic within your expertise can establish you as an authority. It demonstrates your knowledge and credibility, which can instill trust and confidence in your clients.

- **Accessibility:** E-books can be downloaded and read at the reader's convenience, making them an accessible resource for clients. They can refer to the e-book whenever needed, allowing them to absorb the information at their own pace.

- **Value-Added Service:** Offering an e-book as a free download or bonus material can add value to your services. It could also incentivize potential clients to sign up for your therapy sessions or subscribe to your newsletter.

- **Marketing tool**: An e-book can be a powerful marketing tool. It can attract potential clients, encourage email sign-ups, and increase online visibility.
- **Revenue stream:** While many therapists offer e- books for free, they can also be sold as a separate product for an additional income stream.

Topics and Formats of E-books for Therapy Practice:

Topics for e-books should be relevant to your practice and beneficial for your clients. Some possible topics include:

- An introduction to different types of therapy (CBT, DBT, EMDR, etc.)
- A guide on coping strategies for specific mental health conditions.
- Tips for managing stress, anxiety, or depression.
- A handbook on mindfulness and meditation

techniques.

-        A guide to improving communication and relationships.
-    Personal development and self-improvement guides.

As for the format, an e-book should be easy to read and navigate. Here are some formatting tips:

- **Clear and Concise:** Use simple, straightforward language. Break down complex concepts into digestible chunks of information.
- **Structured:** Have a clear structure with chapters or sections. Use headings and subheadings to organize your content.
- **Visual Elements:** Use images, infographics, or diagrams to illustrate points and make your e- book more engaging.
- **Interactive:** Consider adding interactive elements like quizzes, worksheets, or self- reflection prompts.
- **References:** Include references or further reading for readers who want to explore the topic more deeply.

The goal of your e-book should be to provide value to your clients. It should be a resource that enhances their therapy experience and supports their mental health journey.

WAY 3: SOCIAL MEDIA

Snapshot:

Harnessing the power of social media can be a game-changer for therapy practices in this digital age. Platforms like Facebook, Instagram, and LinkedIn offer an incredible opportunity to reach a wider audience, foster engagement, and build a solid online presence. Therapists can use these platforms to share valuable content such as articles, tips, and insights, host live Q&A sessions, and even offer online workshops or webinars.

Doing so demonstrates their expertise, creates a sense of community, and shows their commitment to supporting mental health. Furthermore, social media can facilitate open conversations about mental health, helping to reduce stigma and normalize seeking help. When used effectively, social media can significantly enhance a therapy practice by improving visibility, accessibility, and client connection.

Deep Focus: Leveraging Social Media Features

One of the benefits of social media is education. Therapists can share informative content such as mental health tips, therapy techniques, or the latest research in the field. Regular posting on social media can help raise awareness about mental health issues, reduce stigma, and encourage people to seek help. *Another advantage of social media is brand building. It allows therapists to showcase their unique approach, values, and personality, helping them attract clients who resonate with their brand.*

However, adhering to best practices when using social media in a therapy context is crucial. This includes respecting confidentiality, providing value, engaging with the audience, being consistent, using a professional account, adhering to ethical guidelines, and measuring effectiveness.

The role of social media in therapy practices is multifaceted. It offers therapists a platform to engage with clients, share valuable resources, and promote mental health awareness. Best practices involve maintaining professional boundaries, ensuring ethical conduct, and leveraging the potential of social media to disseminate accurate and helpful information. Therapists can share educational content, mental health tips, and resources on social media. This extends their reach and provides valuable information to a broader audience.

By adhering to best practices, therapists can leverage social media as a powerful tool to provide support and contribute to the broader landscape of mental health education and advocacy.

Deeper Focus: Enhancing Therapy Through Social Media

In the digital era, social media has become an essential contrivance for businesses, including therapy practices. Therapists can utilize social media platforms to connect with a larger audience, engage with clients, share valuable content, and establish a robust online presence.

- **Reach:** Social media platforms have a vast user base, enabling therapists to reach potential clients beyond their local area.

- **Engagement:** Platforms like Facebook, Instagram, or Twitter allow therapists to interact with their audience, answer questions, and facilitate discussions around mental health topics.

- **Education:** Therapists can use social media to share informative content, such as mental health tips, therapy techniques, or the latest research in the field.

- **Awareness:** Regularly posting on social media can help raise awareness about mental health issues, reduce stigma, and encourage people to seek help.

- **Brand Building:** Social media provides an opportunity for therapists to showcase their unique approach, values, and personality, helping them to stand out and attract clients who resonate with their brand.

Best Practices for Using Social Media in a Therapy Context:

- **Respect Confidentiality:** Never share client information on social media. Always maintain professional boundaries and respect your client's privacy and confidentiality.

- **Provide Value:** Share informative, practical, and relevant content to your audience. This could be mental health tips, blog posts, videos, or inspirational quotes.

- **Engage:** Don't just post content; engage with your audience. Respond to comments, answer questions, and participate in relevant discussions.

- **Be Consistent:** Post content regularly to maintain visibility and engagement. However, prioritize quality over quantity. It's better to share fewer high-quality posts than many low-quality ones.

- **Use a Professional Account:** Keep your personal and professional social media accounts separate. This helps maintain professional boundaries and ensures your content reaches the right audience.

- **Be Mindful of Ethical Guidelines:** Ensure your social media use aligns with the ethical guidelines of your professional body. This may include guidelines on advertising, testimonials, dual relationships, and online conduct.

- **Measure Effectiveness:** Use analytics to understand what content resonates with your audience, when the best time to post is, and which platforms are most effective for your practice.

Social media is a tool. Use it wisely and ethically to enhance your therapy practice, provide value to your audience, and promote mental health awareness.

WAY 4: WEBINARS

Snapshot:

Webinars can be a remarkably effective tool for expanding the reach and impact of a therapy practice. These live, online events offer therapists a platform to delve deep into specific mental health topics, providing valuable education and training to clients and a broader audience.

Webinars can be an interactive space for real-time Q&As, discussions, and even group exercises, fostering a sense of community and active participation. They can also be recorded and accessed later, adding to a practice's digital resources. By hosting webinars, therapists can demonstrate their expertise, attract potential clients, and provide additional support to existing clients.

Thus, webinars can significantly enhance a therapy practice by driving engagement, education, and accessibility in a profoundly personal and interactive manner.

Deep Focus: Crafting Engaging Webinars

Marketing webinars can be a great marketing tool, offering free webinars to attract potential clients or paid webinars to provide an additional income stream. To ensure successful webinar hosting, therapists should choose a relevant topic, plan their content, select a reliable platform, promote their webinar using various channels, and test their tech before the webinar.

Engaging the audience during the webinar is crucial, as it helps maintain the connection and enhances their experience. Therapists should also send follow-up emails after the webinar to strengthen the relationship with the audience.

Therapists can use webinars to enhance their therapy practice by providing valuable educational content, fostering client engagement, and extending their reach to a broader audience. Successful webinar hosting in therapy involves careful planning, engaging content, and effective communication.

Therapists should identify the specific goals and objectives of the webinar, ensure that the content aligns with the needs and interests of the target audience, create engaging and interactive content that encourages participation, discussion, and knowledge sharing among participants, and leverage interactive features like live polls, Q&A sessions, and breakout rooms to facilitate meaningful engagement and learning experiences.

By following best practices and leveraging webinars' interactive features, therapists can enhance their therapy practices by providing valuable resources, fostering client engagement, and contributing to the broader mental health education and advocacy field.

Deeper Focus: Enhancing Therapy Through Webinars

Webinars are live online events that allow real-time interaction between a presenter and an audience. Webinars can be a powerful tool for therapy practices to educate clients, reach a wider audience, and showcase a therapist's expertise.

- **Education:** Webinars offer an opportunity to delve deeper into specific topics related to mental health, therapy techniques, self-care strategies, etc. You can use visuals, demonstrations, and real-time Q&A to provide a comprehensive learning experience.
- **Reach:** Webinars are online so that they can be accessed anywhere. This allows therapists to reach potential clients beyond their local area.
- **Engagement:** The interactive nature of webinars allows therapists to engage with their audience in real time. This can foster a sense of community and connection.
- **Brand Building:** Hosting webinars can help establish a therapist as an authority in their field, building credibility and trust with their audience.
- **Marketing:** Webinars can be a great marketing tool. Free webinars can attract potential clients, while paid webinars can provide an additional income stream.

Tips for Successful Webinar Hosting:

1. **Choose a Relevant Topic:** Your webinar topic should appeal to your audience. It could be based on common questions you receive, current mental health trends, or your area of expertise.

2. **Plan Your Content:** Your webinar should have a clear structure, including an introduction, the main content, a Q&A session, and a conclusion.

3. **Choose a Reliable Platform:** There are many webinar platforms available, such as Zoom, GoToWebinar, or Webex. Choose one that is reliable, easy to use, and has the needed features.

4. **Promote Your Webinar:** Promote your webinar using

your website, social media, email newsletters, and other channels. Consider using a registration page to collect attendees' contact information for follow-up.

5. **Test Your Tech:** Before the webinar, ensure that your internet connection, audio, video, and webinar platform are all working correctly. A technical glitch during the webinar can disrupt your attendees' experience.

6. **Engage Your Audience:** Encourage interaction during your webinar by asking questions, encouraging comments, and having a Q&A session.

7. **Follow-Up:** After the webinar, send a follow-up email to attendees with a thank you note, a recap of the webinar, or additional resources. This helps maintain the connection with your audience and enhances their experience.

The success of a webinar depends on the value it provides. Ensure your webinar is informative, interactive, and professionally conducted.

WAY 5: PODCASTS

Snapshot:

Leveraging the power of podcasts can substantially amplify the impact of a therapy practice. Podcasts provide a unique, intimate platform for therapists to discuss mental health topics, share expert insights, and provide practical advice in a format that is easily accessible and consumable for clients and a wider audience.

The conversational nature of podcasts also allows therapists to showcase their personality and approach, facilitating a deeper connection with listeners. They can invite guest speakers, such as mental health advocates or other therapists, to widen the scope of discussion and provide diverse perspectives.

By offering valuable, on-demand content in a personal and engaging way, therapists can position themselves as thought leaders in their field, attract potential clients, and provide ongoing support to existing ones. Therefore, podcasts can significantly enhance a therapy practice by extending reach, fostering connection, and promoting mental health awareness.

Deep Focus: Starting a Therapy-Focused Podcast

To create a successful podcast, therapists should identify specific goals and objectives, ensure that the content aligns with the needs and interests of the target audience, and leverage interactive features such as interviews, expert discussions, and audience Q&A sessions. Effective communication and promotion are crucial to attract listeners and ensure a successful outreach. Therapists should use various communication channels, such as social media, email newsletters, and professional networks, to promote the podcast and encourage audience participation.

Providing clear instructions for accessing the podcast platform and participating in the episodes ensures listeners a seamless and user-friendly experience. By following best practices and leveraging the interactive features of podcasts, therapists can enhance their therapy practice by providing valuable resources, fostering client engagement, and contributing to the broader landscape of mental health education and advocacy.

Podcast Potentials

- **Reach:** Podcasts can be accessed globally, allowing therapists to connect with potential clients beyond their local area.

- **Flexibility:** Podcasts can be consumed anywhere, anytime - during a commute, workout, or lunch break. This flexibility makes them a convenient way for clients to access valuable information.

- **Engagement:** Podcasts are an intimate medium that can create a sense of connection and engagement between the therapist and the listener.

- **Authority:** Hosting a podcast can help establish a therapist as an authority in their field, building credibility and trust with their audience.

- **Marketing:** Podcasts can be an effective marketing tool, helping to raise awareness of a therapist's services, attract new clients, and strengthen relationships with existing clients.

Deeper Focus: Enhancing Therapy Practices through Podcasts

If you are interested in starting a therapy-focused podcast, here are some steps that you can follow to get started:

1. **Define Your Purpose.** What do you want to achieve with your podcast? Possible answers include educating, providing resources, attracting clients, or establishing authority in your field.

2. **Identify Your Audience:** Who are you creating your podcast for? Understanding your audience's needs, interests, and challenges will guide your content creation.

3. **Plan Your Content:** What topics will you cover? Will you have guest interviews? How frequently will you release episodes? Plan your content to align with your purpose and audience's needs.

4. **Choose Your Format:** Will it be a solo podcast, co-hosted, interview-based, or a mix of formats? Each format has strengths, so choose one that suits your style and content.

5. **Get the Right Equipment:** Invest in a good quality microphone to ensure precise audio. You'll also need recording and editing software, which is free.

6. **Record and Edit:** Record your podcast episodes and edit them to ensure a smooth listening experience. If it's within your budget, consider hiring a professional.

7. **Publish and Promote:** Choose a podcast hosting platform to publish your episodes. Promote your podcast on your website,

social media, and other channels to reach your audience.

8.   **Engage with Listeners:** Encourage listener interaction by asking for questions, feedback, or topic suggestions. Respond to comments to foster engagement and build a community around your podcast.

A successful podcast requires consistency, quality content, and listener engagement. Starting a podcast can be a significant undertaking, but with careful planning and execution, it can be a valuable addition to your therapy practice.

WAY 6: INFOGRAPHICS

Snapshot:

Infographics can be a powerful tool to elevate a therapy practice, providing a visually engaging and easily digestible way to convey complex mental health information. Therapists can enhance client understanding and retention of information by presenting data, insights, and therapeutic strategies in a visually compelling format.

Infographics can cover various topics, from explaining mental health disorders and treatment processes to offering self-help techniques and tips. They can be shared on multiple platforms, including social media, blogs, and emails, increasing the practice's visibility and reach.

Additionally, well-designed infographics can reinforce a practice's professional image and showcase the therapist's expertise uniquely and memorably. Thus, infographics can enhance therapy by improving client education, engagement, and communication.

Deep Focus: Crafting Effective Infographics

Keeping the client's needs and capabilities in mind while creating infographics is essential. Effective infographics can improve education, communication, and scientific research and support the development of communication skills.

Therapists should select relevant content, present it clearly and engagingly, consider the format, color schemes, and consistent use of fonts to maintain visual coherence and ensure the information presented is accurate, evidence-based, and aligned with ethical guidelines in therapy practices.

Infographics can be a valuable resource for therapists to enhance education, communication, and client engagement.

By creating visually appealing and informative infographics, therapists can support understanding mental health concepts, promote health literacy, and contribute to the broader landscape of mental health education and advocacy.

Benefits of Using Infographics for Therapy Practices:

- **Simplify Complex Concepts:** Infographics can distill complex ideas or processes into simple visuals, making them easier for clients to understand.
- **Engage and Educate:** Well-designed infographics can grab attention, engage clients, and serve as a valuable educational resource.
- **Enhance Recall:** Visual information is more easily

remembered than text, enhancing the retention of information.

- **Shareable:** Infographics are easily shared across websites, blogs, and social media platforms, increasing your reach and visibility.
- **Versatility:** Infographics can be used in various ways – in blog posts, social media, client handouts, presentations, or email newsletters.

Deeper Focus: Enhancing Therapy Practices through Infographics

Infographics can be a potent tool for presenting information in a visually appealing way. To create efficient infographics, it is essential to keep a few critical tips in mind. By following these guidelines, you can create infographics that grab your audience's attention and effectively convey your message.

1. **Define Your Objective:** What is the key message you want to convey? Having a clear objective will guide the design and content of your infographic.
2. **Keep It Simple:** Don't overload your infographic with too much information. Keep it focused on a single topic or concept.
3. **Use Visuals Effectively:** Use images, charts, and diagrams to represent information visually. Make sure these visuals enhance understanding rather than confuse it.
4. **Organize Information:** Arrange information in a logical flow. Depending on your content, this could be a step-by-step process, a timeline, a comparison, or a list.
5. **Make It Attractive:** Use colors, fonts, and layout effectively to make your infographic visually appealing. However, ensure it remains easy to read and understand.
6. **Cite Sources:** If you're using data or information from other sources, cite them in your infographic.
7. **Test and Revise:** Before sharing your infographic more widely, test it with a small group to get feedback and revise it as

needed.

Creating professional-looking infographics is easier than ever, thanks to free online tools like Canva, Piktochart, or Venngage. Even if you lack design skills, these platforms allow anyone to create an appealing infographic. The primary purpose of an infographic is to enhance understanding, so it should simplify information rather than make it more complex. When creating infographics, always consider your client's needs and capabilities.

WAY 7: ONLINE COURSES

Snapshot:

Online courses can be a game-changer in enhancing the scope and effectiveness of a therapy practice. By providing structured and in-depth courses on various mental health subjects, therapists can offer a comprehensive learning experience beyond traditional therapy sessions.

These courses can cover multiple topics, from understanding specific mental health conditions to learning coping strategies and self-care techniques. They empower clients to actively participate in their healing journey, promoting self-reliance and resilience. Moreover, online courses can help reach a wider audience, expanding the impact of the practice while positioning the therapist as an authority in the field, thus improving their credibility.

Deep Focus: Crafting Valuable Online Courses

The ultimate goal of an online course in a therapy context should be to support clients' therapeutic journey and enhance their understanding of their mental health.

Therapists can help clients better manage their mental health and overall wellness by providing additional resources and knowledge.

Online courses can enhance therapy practice by providing structured, in-depth educational resources, fostering continuous learning, and extending reach to a broader audience.

Therapists should identify specific goals and learning objectives, design practical and evidence- based information, and consider the format, structure, and delivery methods to ensure the content is engaging, accessible, and conducive to learning. This may involve incorporating multimedia elements, interactive exercises, and self-assessment tools to enhance the overall learning experience for participants.

Role of Online Courses in Therapy Practices:

- **Education:** Online courses can provide comprehensive, structured guidance on specific topics related to mental health, self-care, coping mechanisms, and more.
- **Accessibility:** Online courses can be accessed from anywhere, making them a convenient resource for clients.
- **Engagement:** Interactive elements in online courses, such as quizzes or discussion forums, can foster engagement and active learning.
- **Support:** Courses can supplement therapy sessions by providing additional information or exercises to help

clients progress.

- **Revenue:** Therapists can offer online courses as a paid service, opening up an additional revenue stream.

Deeper Focus: Steps to Create a Valuable Online Course for Clients

1. **Identify a Need:** What topics are your clients interested in or struggling with? Use these insights to identify a course topic that will provide value.

2. **Plan Your Course:** Define the course objectives, outline the course content, and decide on the course format (video, text, audio, etc.). Break down the content into manageable modules or lessons.

3. **Create Engaging Content:** To cater to different learning styles, use a mix of teaching methods – this could include text, videos, audio, **infographics, quizzes, and exercises. Make sure the content is clear, concise, and engaging.**

4. **Choose a Platform:** Many online platforms, like Teachable, Udemy, or Kajabi, make it easy to create, host, and sell online courses.

5. **Test Your Course:** Before launching, test your course to ensure everything works smoothly and the content achieves its learning objectives.

6. **Launch and Promote:** Launch your course and promote it through your website, social media, email newsletter, and other channels.

7. **Monitor and Update:** Gather feedback from your clients and use it to improve and update your course as needed.

The goal of an online course in a therapy context should be to support your clients' therapeutic journey and enhance their understanding of their mental health. It should not replace individual therapy but can be a valuable additional resource.

IMPLEMENTATION AND EVALUATION

In today's dynamic mental health world, digital content strategies are vital in revolutionizing therapeutic practices. As therapists increasingly move into the digital realm, these strategies can optimize the delivery of mental health resources and provide a powerful conduit for client engagement and mental health advocacy. By crafting engaging content across diverse digital platforms - from websites to podcasts and online courses - therapists can transcend geographical boundaries, reach a wider audience, and establish themselves as trusted authorities. However, creating and implementing digital content strategies is just the first step; the real power lies in the ongoing process of evaluation and adaptation.

Monitoring the performance and impact of these strategies can yield valuable insights, leading to continuous improvement and, ultimately, enhanced effectiveness of therapy practices in the ever-evolving digital landscape.

Evaluating and Monitoring Digital Content:

The importance of monitoring and evaluating the effectiveness of your digital content cannot be overstated. It helps you understand what's working and what's not and how to improve your content strategy.

1.   **Use Analytics:** Most digital platforms provide analytics that can give you insights into how your content is performing. This could include the number of views, likes, shares, comments, time spent on a page, etc.

2.   **Measure Engagement:** Engagement metrics, like comments, shares, and likes, can indicate how your audience interacts with your content.

3.   **Monitor Conversions:** Conversions could be the number of new clients, email sign-ups, course enrollments, etc. This can help you understand if your content is effectively driving desired actions.

4.   **Gather Feedback:** Ask your audience for feedback on your content. This can give you insights into what they find helpful, what they want more of, and how you can improve.

5.   **Review and Adjust:** Use the information gathered from analytics, engagement, conversions, and feedback to review and adjust your content strategy.

Digital content is not a 'set it and forget it' strategy. It requires ongoing monitoring, evaluation, and adjustment to ensure it continues to meet your goals and provide value to your audience.

FINAL REMARKS

In today's digital age, therapists use digital content to improve their practice and connect with clients. Technology can expand the reach of therapy, enabling personalized care and facilitating connection. Webinars, podcasts, and social media posts are just a few tools therapists can use to broaden their visibility, improve client relationships, and optimize their services. By receiving technology training and thoughtfully implementing digital tools, therapists can easily navigate the ever-evolving digital landscape.

Therapists can strengthen patient engagement and deepen their relationships with existing and potential clients by leveraging high-quality, search- engine-optimized content, interactive digital resources, and personalized approaches.

As therapy evolves with technology, therapists must embrace digital content to remain competitive. High-quality, interactive digital content that caters to client needs can build therapists' credibility, showcase their expertise, and position them as industry leaders. Digital tools also enable social engagement opportunities for better conversations between clients and therapists.

Technology has potential applications in improving interventions and adherence, making it essential for therapists to gain proficiency in digital technology.

The future of therapy is on the brink of transformation, and therapists must make the most of this opportunity to provide meaningful treatments that foster positive change in our world.

By embracing digital content, therapists can reach a wider audience, increase trust and credibility, foster meaningful engagement with clients, and make therapy delivery more efficient. Crafting carefully crafted, optimized content that reflects their expertise and values allows therapists to surge ahead in the digital landscape and impact the lives of many.

Contact us today to navigate the digital landscape with ease. We'll help you broaden your reach, deepen client relationships, and enhance your practice. Make a lasting impact with your digital content.

You can order all types of original content with the 100% free

Contact us today to navigate the digital landscape with ease. We'll help you broaden your reach, deepen client relationships, and enhance your practice. Make a lasting impact with your digital content.

You can order all types of original content with the 100% free